242

Bread - Religious aspects

Becoming
Bread

Also by Gunilla Norris

Being Home: A Book of Meditations (1991)

Becoming

Bread

Meditations on Loving
and Transformation

Gunilla Norris

Drawings by John Giuliani

BELL TOWER New York

Published by Bell Tower, an imprint of Harmony Books,
a division of Crown Publishers, Inc., 201 East 50th Street,
New York, New York 10022. Member of the Crown
Publishing Group.

Random House, Inc. New York, Toronto, London, Sydney,
Auckland.

Bell Tower and colophon are registered trademarks of
Crown Publishers, Inc.

Manufactured in the United States of America

Designed by Marjorie Anderson

Library of Congress Cataloging-in-Publication Data

Norris, Gunilla Brodde, 1939–
    Becoming bread : meditations on loving and
transformation /
    Gunilla Norris ; drawings by John Giuliani. — 1st ed.
        1. Bread—Religious aspects—Christianity—
Meditations.   2. Love—Religious aspects—
Christianity—Meditations.   I. Title.
BV825.52.N67 1993
242—dc20   92-19259
                                                      CIP

ISBN 0-517-59168-5
10 9 8 7 6 5 4 3 2 1
First Edition

This book is dedicated to the source of all relationships, with gratitude for Jennifer, John, Dobritte, and Chloe, treasured friends, and in memory of Lee, who shared his bread with grace.

Contents

Acknowledgments

Many thanks to Toinette Lippe, not only for her skill as an editor but also for her longtime dedication to publishing spiritually useful books. I want to thank my son, John, and the following friends for thoughtfully responding to the manuscript in whole or in part: Platt Arnold, Lee Brunner, Carolyn Dukenski, Danit Freid, Greg Johanson, Ro King, Howard Lawrence, Florence Phillips, Greta Sibley, Norman Sibley, Joyce Sievers, Gail Straub, and Ellen Wingard. My thanks also to my agent, Bob Silverstein, for his encouragement. I want to give additional thanks to Greta Sibley, whose wonderful design ideas have helped me "see" the book. And my gratitude to Marjorie Anderson, who did the final graceful design, and to John Giuliani for his lovely drawings.

Preface

For a long time I have wanted to write a book about loving. I have wanted to do this as a continuing question—an inquiry really, because good questions sometimes carry answers on their backs.

Love for me has been a powerful question . . . one asked even more penetratingly after my marriage of twenty-eight years ended. In those years I loved much and so did my husband. Yet the relationship ended. I have loved family and friends and I have been loved by them. Some of these relationships have reached depths I could not have dreamed of. Grace became visible and changed me forever. Other relationships have stayed on the surface, pleasantly skipping along like flat stones. And some have been devastating.

Why is this? Why is love so nourishing and yet so painful? How can it be everywhere? How can it also be so elusive? What can we say about it? Love—so varied, so strange, and so common. How do we receive this gift?

Perhaps we cannot rightly love each other or ourselves unless we love God. Perhaps the truth is that we cannot love God unless we love ourselves and each other. Is love ever understood except through experience? I don't know how to answer these questions. But they feel life-giving to me. And I want to spend the rest of my life trying to find the answers to them.

To ask is to question as well as to request, to claim, to expect, to need, and to call for. This book is part of my asking and I hope you will join me with your asking. I think we have all felt that we become more fully ourselves when we love and are loved. We know that love nourishes us. When it is in our lives, we can bear pain, confusion, and even death. This is why I link the food of the spirit, love, and the food of the body, bread. Both are staples. They sustain us.

Beginning

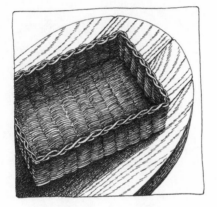

Bread on a journey is no burden.

Russian proverb

We do not need to own a kitchen or spend time in one to know the significance of bread. We need never see a bread recipe or try our hand at baking to realize that bread is a profound and ancient symbol for life. To grow grain and to store it guaranteed our ancestors the possibility of survival. The oldest grain cereal known to man was the common wheat native to the prehistoric plains of Asia. It was cultivated by the Stone Age man of the Neolithic period. Here was the beginning of bread.

Flour and salt—the makings of bread—were frequently brought to our early altars. The sacrifices were made in recognition of the fact that we are fundamentally creatures of need. These offerings were petitions for sustenance. We have understood from the beginning how dependent and vulnerable we are. We have known that in order to live we will always have to receive and care for the gifts of life.

And we have also known that we must share these gifts. They are not for us alone. Hoarded, they molder just as uneaten bread molders. We must share life, share bread with each other. We are each given only so much time. And to make this time matter, in order to really live, we need to give, we need to receive. We need to love. Bread, life, and love are fused in the soul of human experience.

Our religious and philosophical texts are filled with references to bread, and proverbs about it abound in our folk wisdom. Holidays and family events are marked by the eating of festive breads to commemorate these special moments. We share bread at almost every meal, forgetting how old this is in us.

Deep in our souls we know that *we* are the bread of life and that to become conscious of this and to live it makes all the difference . . . it frees us to be more truly human and to care for each other.

Becoming Bread is a book of meditations for sharing with someone we love and cherish. It asks the reader to see the steps of making bread as the unfolding process of self-knowledge, of growing communion with a loved one, and of surrender to the huge context in which we dwell. None of this can be hurried, just as making bread cannot be hurried.

When a loaf of bread is taken out of the oven, it is hot and moist. It is laid on the breadboard and the kitchen fills with yeasty fragrance. Much has happened for this bread to have come into being. And more will continue to happen.

We smell the bread. We see its brown patina and touch the crust. Warmth comes into our fingertips. We experience the bread as we do our loving . . . with all of our senses. To be here, on the breadboard, this loaf has gone through the fire. Soon it will be consumed and give nourishment. And soon it will also be forgotten.

When we look at the loaf we may think how we, too, must go through fire to become ourselves, to become sustenance for each other and for life itself. We are each part of this mystery. This is how life has always been, how it has manifested itself in the universe—becoming, sustaining, and surrendering to become again another way, another time.

Love. Bread. It breaks. It crumbles. It nourishes. We share it. Bread that comes from grain, from earth, from rain, from summer and light, from labor and threshing. Bread of comfort, of necessity, of sorrow. Bread that brings life. Fresh bread. Stale bread. Bread crumbs. We are all of that.

The potential for a loving relationship with ourselves, with each other, and with God is a gift. We cannot *make* it. But we can choose to be oriented toward the only place loving can occur, namely right here, now, where we are. Just the living of that orientation makes it more possible for this gift, this blessing, to happen to us and for us to receive it. Each time we share bread with each other, we symbolize this mystery.

Perhaps only sages can truly speak about loving and how it transforms us. We are not sages. We are ordinary people. I hope that this ordinariness will be a good enough credential to entitle any of us to speak from the heart. And to speak boldly even as we know that we do not really know. For here, together, we are becoming, becoming something which is not yet apparent. Dough does not know what is being made of it. Yet bread possesses an absolute integrity. Perhaps we can accept that unknowing is a blessing, for then we can be transformed, we can become something "for God."

Place

The field is God's table.

Estonian proverb

Making bread is as mysterious as loving and yet it is something anyone can do. To make bread we know we need some kind of kitchen. To love we know we must meet each other *somewhere*. We know that place of meeting is none other than the here and now. There is no meeting anywhere else. We cannot live separately from what is.

We are given bodies. We are given the world. We are given time. But without attention, without awareness, without true presence, we do not meet, we do not find each other. There is no "kitchen."

In the here and now dwells the truth that all of us are limited . . . that we are continuously moving and changing . . . always longing and reaching for the not-yet. The truth is that we are the energy in these bodies, burning through time . . . that we are dying. This is fundamental—our earth, our water, our air, and our fire.

Let us meet where we already are, in the elements of our vulnerability. In this we are together and we cannot do without each other. This is basic. Our neighbor is our self.

The Kitchen

Familiar and strange,
the kitchen is a holy place—
alive with possibility.

A place for the elements.
Water in the tap,
fire in the stove,
earth in the food,
air—between, around, above, and below.

Behind the cupboard doors
are the pots and the pans,
the bowls and the dishes,
the measuring cups
and the measuring spoons—

holy things
that lie ready for use,
much like our dreams
that lie waiting
behind our eyelids.

The kitchen is alchemical,
a place where we cook—actually
and spiritually. We come to it
for nourishment and ease.
We come to it as to a center—

the heart of the house,
the heart of dwelling.
In the kitchen we are one,
linked by hunger—
actual hunger and spiritual hunger.

We go to the kitchen to be
nourished and revealed.
It is a holy place.

At the Threshold

Stand at the kitchen door with me.
Honor the heart of transformation.
Honor your own heart
where everything is
always changing.
It is the very same dwelling.

Pause at the door.
Your heart needs this.
My heart needs this time
for recognition or it will go astray.
It will forget to reach for
its real joy . . . its true becoming.

Pause at the door.
This is good and necessary
for this room is *every* room.
The world lives here.
Pausing each day helps us know
nothing is outside of us.

Honor the heart that can feel
the joy and the terror of
the world in you and in me.
Only what is truly human
can walk this path, walk through
and be constant. Bow to *that* heart.

Hold my hand. I need you for courage.
We become who we are together,
each needing the other. Alone is a myth.
The path leads through this door.
I cannot go to the kitchen without you.
Let us enter together.

Willingness

Hunger teaches us many things.

Irish proverb

Not only do we need a kitchen to bake bread, we need the will to be engaged in the process. This is true of loving also. Without the will to love, we cannot be consistent. "Love is a direction and not a state of the soul," as Simone Weil says.

But there is a tension here, for will can as easily be willful as it can be willing. And there is a vast difference between the two. Most often willfulness is based on fear. We try to make the world the way we want it by forcing solutions. Compensating for the uncertainty inside us, we become motivated by power instead of participation. Then we find struggles instead of solutions because force is often met with resistance. We stay emotionally hungry yet cannot be fed. We ask for more and more, and receive less. Willingness, on the other hand, allows life to show us the way.

"Thy will be done," we say in the Lord's Prayer. And the very next line is, "Give us this day our daily bread." Truly prayed, this is a prayer of willingness . . . willingness to desire God's will. Willingness to feel and recognize hunger and therefore willingness to receive sustenance. Willingness to forgive and be forgiven. This prayer understands our human nature.

When we can open the cupboard door in the heart's kitchen, we are expressing this acceptance of creatureliness. As we look at the ingredients inside . . . the ones we like and the ones we prefer to deny . . . we are beginning to trust God to make bread out of all that. The outcome won't be up to us, but we will be participating. We will begin to "intend to make the service of love a beautiful thing," as the twelfth-century Beguine, Hadewijch of Antwerp, tells us, "Want nothing else, fear nothing else, and let love be free to become what love truly is."

Water

In this heart place there is order
and disorder. Riptides. Storms
and dead calm. Here in the kitchen
we find a sea of unknown feelings.

We are born in these waters.
We bear each other in them.
Beginning again . . . like waves . . .
outgoing . . . incoming . . .
orderless order . . . deep water.

This place is innocent and wild.
It is our own moods and weather
we find here. When I am calm, you are
orderless. When you sort, I disorganize.

We cannot reassure each other
in these storms. Between the counters
there is foul weather and what we have
relied on in each other floats away.

Finding love here in the outgoing . . .
incoming tide . . . we must begin again
to trust and so take up unknowing
as a way, a truthful pattern.

We bear ourselves for the sake of the other.
We bear the other for the sake of ourselves.
The truth we have not dared to live yet
deepens here . . . fathomless water.

The Mixing Bowl

Here on the table
is the mixing bowl.
Brown and ordinary,
turned on the potter's wheel,
it has an umber rim
and glazed, cinnamon-speckled sides.

Its task is to be open,
a simple space. This bowl is
clay, earth, matter. Particular.
We are like it. Clay,
earth, matter. Particular
and vast when we are empty . . .

when life can fill us
to the rim, brimming.
We are the mixing place
where terror and hate,
where love and hope,
the way we move,

our smiles and uncertainties,
our courage and stupidities
are all embraced.
We are the body bowl . . .
the forming space,
the home of possibility.

Hunger

In this place hunger is our guide.
What shall we find here to nourish us?
We have nothing of our own . . .
nothing but need.

I forage for the pans.
You bring out the bowl.
The cups gape—wide
like open mouths. Hungry.

These things are empty.
Let us be like them . . . begging
to be filled. This hunger is our gift.
The one we want

to look away from. The one we hide
from one another. Let me learn
to love you in your want. I beg you
to love the hunger that is mine.

Do not seek to allay it. Do not be afraid.
Protect my hunger with love
for then I shall find the way to become
real bread. And you shall be fed.

Discover the grain that hides in your hunger,
the one that can be worked into a loaf,
and I shall feast on your joy.
Light a light so that we see the emptiness

of the pot and the pan, the emptiness
in the curve of the spoon, the emptiness
in the shape of your hand that can cradle
my hunger and yet not take it from me.

In this gift of sheltering I will find
that my hunger is life hungering for itself
and that I can trust that hunger, receive it
as my truth, as myself.

Bowls and cups, pots and pans,
spoons—my hand, your hand.
We shall come to know ourselves
as vessels that can hold this moment

for each other, for the greater life
that seeks itself in us, trusts us and
hungers in us. Let us be vessels . . .
openings . . . sheltering space.

Seeing

"Bread," we say,
looking at one another. "Bread,"
we say, looking at ourselves.

There is flour in the cupboard,
salt, and honey—the ingredients
of bread on the shelves. Here

I may find what I was afraid to see.
Here you may see what you didn't know
you had. The risk of knowing

is here in the cupboard. . . .
How little we have dared to use ourselves.
How much has been kept from each other.

"Bread," we say. "Let me see
inside the cupboard. Let me
look behind the door."

I am afraid when you can see
what I would not look at
for then I must know myself.

On the shelf the sack
we call flour might be empty,
might be full of miller moths—unusable.

On the shelf there might be
bounty—sacks and sacks of wheat,
and I could feel the shame of riches,

a terrible abundance that could tear us
apart. Make a rift. You poor . . . me rich
and therefore both in poverty.

I am afraid when you see
what I would not look at.
Your eyes are my witness.

If they look with love
I can bear to see what I have to offer—
the grain of my experience . . . my flour.

Gifts

You can think as much as you like
but you will invent nothing better
than bread and salt.

Russian proverb

To make bread we have to take the ingredients out of the cupboard and assemble them so they can be seen and used. We have to know and understand what is there.

What *is* there? The earth under our feet. The water in our glasses. The simple tastes of sweet and salt. The seasons. The very rhythm of life. The list can go on. We are grounded in these basic gifts.

We do not appreciate these gifts unless we recognize them . . . and recognize them repeatedly. They are the manna, the daily bread from heaven. New each day. To be used each day. "Be ready at all times for the gifts of God and always for new ones," says Meister Eckhart. They are given to us even if we don't receive them. They are the continual ingredients of our lives.

But when we do receive them, when we honor the goodness around us, we sense that we are released from our narrow self-absorbed view. A midrash tells us that "when the world was created God made everything a little bit incomplete. Rather than making bread grow right out of the earth, God made wheat grow so that we might bake it into bread. In this way we could become partners in completing the work of creation."

Recognition. Repetition. Reverence. Receiving. These are ways we grow to know that we ourselves are integral parts of the whole. We, too, are manna.

Spring

We open the bags.
The flour lies there
soft and brown—grain
we can touch—grain
we can smell and use.

The wheat has Spring in it.
Even now it contains
those early plantings, the growth
reaching forward into time,
into a future harvest—this flour.

I want to remember your Spring
as constant . . . as here in this wheat.
I want to think of you young.
I want to think of me beginning . . .
both of us reaching into earth,

into the future, rooting into life,
where we meet now—where we are
asking for nourishment . . . asking
to become bread for one another. As we sift
this fine flour I want to feel you greening.

Earth

Your wheat grew in the ground as did mine.
We have no experience without soil.
Background—our parents and their parents.
Home-ground—our feet on this earth.

Made from ground, sustained by ground,
we are soil. This is the first humility.
If we forget this, we forget that we are human.
We are of the land. We are humus.

Measuring

Made of glass, the measuring cup
is transparent. It holds and it measures
as in music. There is a rhythm here—
a rightness . . . something tempered.

It is not good for a melody to rush
beyond its tempo. So, too, in bread.
The water must be measured.
Two cups and a little more.

One for you and one for me
and some for the stranger . . .
the one we do not know in ourselves.
Pour the water . . . the living measure

into the mixing bowl—love's alembic.
Not too much. Not too little. Let it fall.
Let it seek its level. Let it run from the well,
into the bowl . . . sufficient to the heart.

Salt

Add the salt. A tablespoon of flavor.
Salt from the sea. Salt from the mountain.
Salt from the body . . .
salt after our tears have dried . . .
the residue of grief and frustration.
In time this salt will preserve us.

Add the salt after sweat,
after effort. What our work has
asked of us again and again.
Over time this salt will preserve us
and our memory of movement . . .
our memory of engagement.

Add the salt after running,
after play, after the joy of games.
Add the salt after sex,
after the mystery of union. . . .
Add this body salt, this life salt.
Dissolve it in the bowl, in water.

Summer

Let the golden honey run
out of the jar. Let the water
be sweetened in our mixing bowl.

Three giant spoonfuls
of Summer—nectar, sunshine,
the hum of bees, warm nights,

and ourselves in the grass.
Three giant spoonfuls of Summer
sweetening the water in the mixing bowl.

We need this liquid gold
to remember the goodness
of life . . . the taste of honey.

The memory of Summer . . .
that it returns, that at the center
the open flower is sweet.

That at the center
when it opens, we too are sweet,
and love, like a swarm of bees,

can fly into us . . . ecstatic,
nectar-drunk and
powdered with pollen.

Our bread will have this
poured-from-the-center
rich gold . . . three giant spoonfuls.

Yeast

When the yeast is added
we will see in the honey water
the unpredictable, the alive . . .
which we can never own or
truly understand. We will see
how it bubbles and froths—
how it rises up—and we will know
that we do not have control. . . .

When the yeast is added
to the sweet and the salty,
the skin-temperature,
warm-blooded water, we will sense
the irrepressible and how it moves
into the very cells of our bodies,
into the blood and marrow. We are
flesh and we are vulnerable. . . .

When the yeast is added—
the impulsive, the unmanageable,
the free—we know we will be
moved. Every part of the mixture!
The inert lump of dough will come alive,
will expand and yield. We will be lifted
out of ourselves, beyond ourselves.
We will be worked. . . .

Autumn

The flour in the sack is soft—
a powdered silk. It is beautiful.
It has become this way
because it was harvested, because
it was threshed, and then milled.

Here is the terror of Autumn.
And the beauty! What is ripe *is*
sacrificed. Torn loose. The grain
is wrested from the plant, from everything
familiar. We must expect this to happen

to ourselves. I want to know this in you . . .
that you have been on the threshing floor.
I need you to see that I have been
between the grinding stones. It will make us
careful of each other, of all grain.

The flour in the sack is soft—
a powdered silk. How terrible is beauty.
How full of sacrifice and grace.
Let us honor all that has dared
to grow to fruition.

Living

The crop of the field is always rich in hope.

Spanish proverb

Once the ingredients are assembled, once they are mixed together into a dough, they will become part of each other. They will be one thing. Life . . . becoming bread . . . becoming life.

Process. We can smile at the pictures we have of it in our minds. Still lives—particular moments in their gilded frames. And yet we know experience is something else. It moves! And we are in it.

In a single day there are thousands of changes. We are confused by them, delighted by them, upset by them, dreaming toward them, rejecting them, longing for them, making predictions for the future about them. We live in our thoughts instead of our lives. If we were truly living we would experience what Pierre Teilhard de Chardin wrote: that "by matter we are nourished, lifted up, linked to everything else, invaded by life."

There is no other way than presence and engagement, participation and compassion. Loving the whole, learning as we go, living as we live. "Once you know how the dough becomes bread, you will understand enlightenment," said Shunryu Suzuki, Roshi. We have to be willing to be dough in order to become bread. There is no other way.

Mixing Dough

Now the flour is added.
Watch it start to be
absorbed in the sweet and salty
water, the yeast-milky water.

Watch the critical moment
when suddenly there is a shift.
Now the flour begins
to absorb the water. God's love

works this way. At first
we are dissolved in it
and then we begin to absorb it
. . . becoming substantial.

We do not know how this happens.
Turned, mixed, and stretched,
made pliable. God-infused,
we are asked to be dough.

On the Counter

Taken out, exposed
on the counter,
I am being kneaded.

The air pounded
out of me,
I am turned

inside out. Rolled over
as if by a breaker.
Beached . . .

I am in the open.
Do not leave me now.
Do not hurt me

or give advice.
Do not rescue me.
Do not stop this.

It is my true chance.
Upside down I may
take shape. I may become

more of myself,
resilient. Let this happen.
Here on the counter

kneaded, turned on end
I will become *less*
and somehow more myself.

Hold my hand.
Do nothing. Soon
it may happen. Soon

I may be kneaded into shape,
smooth, all of one piece,
able to dream forward again.

Soon you may join me
here on the counter.
And I will know you as myself.

Rising

Here in the bowl
is warmth and time to rest.
The dough is set apart and covered.

Here in the bowl
the rising starts
and creeps up the sides

reaching into time,
into space . . . into possibility.
Dreams are like this,

full of air,
going ahead of us,
wanting to take us

beyond the rim
of our horizon,
wanting to lift us out

of where we are.
Dreams are like this . . . unfolding
a moment at a time,

expanding us, breathing us,
demanding something new,
wanting to take shape.

This is also dangerous
for there are dark dreams, terrible
dreams. And the ones where

love asks the impossible from us.
Can this be the restlessness
of God? Are we being dreamed?

Discipline

Live within your harvest.

Persian proverb

After the dough is mixed and kneaded, it grows light with air. Slowly the yeast does its work and the dough rises in the bowl to be punched down and kneaded again. Then it is divided and the bread pans are filled. The dough rises a second time in the individual pans.

We must work with time and with patience if we want to make bread. There is no point in making it if we do not accept this. This is true of loving also.

Awareness . . . acceptance . . . patience. It takes everything we have to be able to live this way. It means that we finally take up what is ours to do and let go of what is beyond our abilities. Life corrects us if we do not learn this. As Montaigne put it, "Greatness of soul consists not so much in soaring high and in pressing forward, as in knowing how to adapt and limit oneself." Einstein was more wry. He said, "The only rational way of educating is to be an example—if one can't help it, a warning example." These lessons cannot be skipped. They are rigorous and yet ultimately kind.

Our natures have organic rules that are innate and God-given. To live by those rules is essential—a discipline, a necessity. Perhaps

a better word is *obedience*. No one can tell us
how to obey our natures except our natures.
It takes self-control . . . a profound way of
attending to our deepest truth. Can we love
each other this way? Can we give each other
time and awareness? Can we help each other
listen? Can we help each other hear?

Punching Down

To think we know the dream God has
placed in us . . . to think we know
how to make it happen. . . . Let this be
punched down. Let this be the Winter blow.

God trusts us—fills our lungs, fills
our bodies, fills our lives. We are God's
dough. If we think this is our doing,
let the punch come—the Winter blow.

God trusts us—fills our cells, fills
our thoughts, moves with our gestures.
If we believe this is our doing,
let the punch come—the Winter blow.

So profoundly does God trust us,
we are asked to return trust with trust,
with true unknowing. A Winter faith,
a blessed darkness where God is at rest

in us. Where we can be at rest in God.
All separation gone. Punch down all
but this enjoyment . . . living without
a why. Living *with* living—a Winter faith.

On the Counter Again

Taken out, exposed
and cold on the counter,
you are being kneaded.

The air pounded
out of you,
you are turned

inside out. Rolled over
in waves.
Everything made visible

on the counter.
I will not leave you now.
I will not hurt you

or give advice.
I will not rescue you.
I will not stop this.

It is your true chance.
Upside down you may
take shape. You may become

more of yourself,
resilient. Let this happen.
Here on the counter

pounded, turned on end.
You will become *less*
and somehow more yourself.

I hold your hand
and do nothing. Soon
it may happen.

You will be kneaded
into shape, smooth,
able to go on again.

We are together here
on the counter and alone.
You will know me as *yourself*.

Shaping

No sooner complete
than incomplete—
All of a piece—then divided.
Torn in half—in thirds and quarters.

To become a loaf
the dough must be given shape.
Set apart. Torn apart.

We must bear this process,
the separation, the aloneness,
the truth that we are singular.
We cannot escape ourselves.

This is suffering
which must be borne or it will be
borne by others . . . more dreadfully.

We are revealed in our solitude
and look at the world
from that place, that vastness. . . .
Your eyes tell me you are infinite.

Limits

The pans are ready.
Their metal edges gleam.
They are greased and floured.
They are ready to hold *just so much* dough.

There is nothing personal here.
This restriction must happen
the way death must happen.
It *is* the way.

Our lives depend on limits.
Our skins first. Our parents—
just those two. Our homes.
Our loves, our work, our friends.

Our talents and our appalling lacks.
Our very breath. In. Out.
The lungs' capacity. No more.
Only so much can be lived!

The pans have limits,
and the dough will grow within them.
This is dependable and good.
A mercy.

The Second Rising

God longs for God
and uses us,
rises in us . . .
becomes in us.

Let us be silent,
a quiet dough

where God moves
into every pore . . .
where God lives
as God pleases.

Let us rise simply.
A quiet dough.

Pain

Bread is relief for all kinds of grief.

Spanish proverb

The dough is put in the oven. Our lives are put to the test. The heat is on. Simone Weil tells us, "When an apprentice gets hurt, or complains of being tired, the workmen and peasants have this fine expression: 'It is the trade entering his body.' Each time that we have some pain to go through, we can say to ourselves quite truly that it is the universe, the order and beauty of the world, and the obedience of creation of God that are entering our body."

Yet the fire can seem unbearable. Feelings burn hot and so very precisely. The place where we hurt the most is also where the greatest possibilities lie. Pain wakes us up.

When those we love are in the fire and we can only watch, it is terrible. We feel helpless and afraid. When we are in the fire and no escape is possible, we tremble and shrink back. The passage through and into the heat of life is what we want . . . what we dread. "Who never ate his bread with tears, who never sat weeping on his bed during care-ridden nights knows you not, you heavenly powers," said Goethe.

Yet our pains can and do begin to heal in the cauterizing flame, in the heat of becoming. We wait with those we love when they are there. We try to trust their pain and ours. Can we bear it? Can we somehow let it have its way?

Fire

In the oven. In the pitch black
of the heat, of the sealed fire.
In the oven we are taken
out of ourselves,
into the unbearable . . .

that place where
all hope dies, where
dreams are stunned
out of existence.
Heat. No thought possible.
No breath. No help.

No direction known.
No rescue available.
Nothing but fire.
It is what we are,
what we become. Nothing.
God's heat or nothing.

Waiting

In this darkness
the minutes shrink us,
the seconds dry us out.

Time is an enemy.
When will this suffering be over?
When will it finish?

You are there, helpless.
My hand goes out
but does not bring relief.

I am there, helpless.
Your eyes fill with tears
and you cannot help me.

The pain lives in us.
It is our particular pain.
Necessary pain. We wait on it.

When will it be done?
When will it be finished?
The minutes bake us.

Dry time, mini-seconds,
time-as-it-ticks-time.
It forges us.

We wait on it and long
for God's time—
Time within time.

Standing Free

The knife scrapes along
the metal edge of the pan.
The bread moves.

It is free. And yet
it holds its shape.
This is a mystery.

Brown and fragrant,
the limits are within it now.
The loaf can stand on its own.

In this way we become
ourselves also. Able to stand.
Free. Together. And alone.

This is a mystery.
We find ourselves *here*
side by side. Warm. Newly born.

Sharing

Even crumbs are bread.

Danish proverb

We are united through sharing . . . our lives made meaningful . . . made new. "Take. Eat. This is my body," said Jesus when He broke the bread at the Last Supper. Then He gave His life for us. Behind all communion is the knowledge that we must give our lives to each other, for each other.

And when we do, we can celebrate, we can mourn, we can trust, we can forgive, we can treasure, we can face our deaths. By sharing we are transformed and come to understand with Meister Eckhart that "all bread is *ours* and is given to me, to others through me, and to me through others. For not only bread but all things necessary for sustenance in this life are given on loan to us with others and to others through us."

In sharing, the meaning of our lives is given back to God.

The One who gives.
The One who receives.
The One who is.

Cooling

So close to the heat,
to the transforming fire,
the bread must now rest.
The loaves need to breathe

on the cooling rack.
They fill the air
with their fragrance,
with the smell of

comfort, the recollection
that there is sometimes plenty,
that we will be nourished,
and that we, too, are food.

We can meet now.
We can come together
to nourish and to receive,
to break bread.

Texture

Hold the bread in your hand—
feel its texture—the integrity of it!

Take the bread in your hand,
and then give it away. Give

the crunch of the crust, and
the softness of the center.

Give the hardness of the heel,
and the crispness of the crumbs.

Give it all. This is life which nourishes
as we give it all away.

Breaking Bread

Break the loaf.
See the miracle
that the bread
springs back at you!

Light and full of air.
Held together with earth
and water. Warmed with fire.
Moist and fragrant.

Receive this bread
and break it.
It is you.
It is me.

It is us together.
It is whole.
It is broken.
Receive this bread.

Crumbs

Be careful with the crumbs.
Do not overlook them.

Be careful with the crumbs:
the little chances to love,

the tiny gestures, the morsels
that feed, the minims.

Take care of the crumbs:
a look, a laugh, a smile,

a teardrop, an open hand. Take care
of the crumbs. They are food also.

Do not let them fall.
Gather them. Cherish them.

Plenty

Having shared our bread,
we know that we are
no longer hungry. It is enough

that you see me for myself.
That I see you for yourself.
That we bless what we see

and do not borrow, do not use
one another. This is how we know
we are no longer hungry . . . that

the world is full of terror, full of beauty
and yet we are not afraid to find solace here.
To be bread for each other. To love.

Savoring

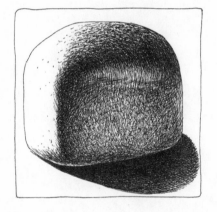

God's hand is always opening.

Spanish proverb

To take nothing for granted and to receive much, this changes everything, makes us empty, makes us new. It transforms us. All gratitude comes from this, that we truly *receive* our lives, each other, and the world.

Time and space. Air and fire. Earth and water. The hot and the dry. Spring and Summer. The cold and the moist. Fall and Winter. Sight. Sound. Touch and smell. Mercy. Terror. Limitation. Pain. When we receive all of it, the whole of life's beauty . . . it *is* bread . . . it is love and we can pray the ancient prayer, "Holy One of Blessing, Your Presence fills creation, bringing forth bread from the earth."

Being human and ordinary, we will often fail to love the whole, the dark and difficult parts. We will always try to avoid something. We will tremble. We will be blind. We will be uncertain. We will continue to hurt one another and miss the essential. We will always need mercy and compassion. We will be ineffective, stubborn, and very human. It is ultimately our vulnerability and our powerlessness that God loves the most, I believe. For there we can and do receive, *must receive*, and know that everything is a gift. Even our suffering.

Full of that knowledge, that sustenance, we cannot help but share our love and our lives with each other. Then we are not only becoming bread . . . we *are* bread.

Beginning Again

Here is the kitchen.
Will you enter it with me?
Let us share the heart of the house.

Here dwelling and becoming
are like angels to wrestle with.
Here limitation will be our friend

and we can grow into love,
into bread. You, a sustenance for me,
and I, a sustenance for you.

Both of us fostered by
the measuring cup, shaped by
the teaspoon and the quarter-teaspoon.

Here the shining world grows
more transparent in its beauty each day.
We are disappearing in its light,

turning into the moment's bright copper,
surrendering to what we do not know
. . . what we cannot see or touch.

Here is the kitchen. Here let us become
the very nourishment we long for.
Becoming what we *are*, unknowing,

light, praise, shared bread. . . .
A living way.

About the Author

Gunilla Norris lives in Newtown, Connecticut, where she works as a writer and psychotherapist in private practice. She is the author of *Being Home: A Book of Meditations*, eleven children's books, and one book of poems, *Learning from the Angel*.

About the Illustrator

John Giuliani is a monk of the Benedictine Grange, West Redding, Connecticut.

Other Bell Tower Books

*The pure sound of the bell
summons us into the present moment.
The timeless ring of truth is expressed
in many different voices, each one magnifying
and illuminating the sacred.
The clarity of its song resonates within us
and calls us away from those things
which often distract us—that which was, that which
might be—to That Which Is.*

BEING HOME: *A Book of Meditations*
by Gunilla Norris
Photographs by Greta D. Sibley

An exquisite modern book of hours, a celebration of
mindfulness in everyday activities.
Hardcover 0-517-58159-0 (1991)

NOURISHING WISDOM
A New Understanding of Eating
by Marc David

A practical way out of dietary confusion, a book that
reveals how our attitude to food reflects our attitude
to life.
Hardcover 0-517-57636-8 (1991)

SANCTUARIES: THE NORTHEAST
*A Guide to Lodgings in Monasteries, Abbeys, &
Retreats of the United States*
by Jack and Marcia Kelly

The first in a series of regional guides for those in
search of renewal and a little peace.
Softcover 0-517-57727-5 (1991)

GRACE UNFOLDING
Psychotherapy in the Spirit of the Tao-te ching
by Greg Johanson and Ron Kurtz

The interaction of client and therapist illuminated
through the gentle power and wisdom
of Lao Tzu's ancient Chinese classic.
Hardcover 0-517-58449-2 (1991)

SELF-RELIANCE
*The Wisdom of Ralph Waldo Emerson
as Inspiration for Daily Living*
Selected and with an introduction by Richard Whelan

A distillation of Emerson's essential spiritual writings
for contemporary readers.
Softcover 0-517-58512-X (1991)

COMPASSION IN ACTION
Setting Out on the Path of Service
by Ram Dass and Mirabai Bush

Heartfelt encouragement and advice for those ready
to commit time and energy to relieving suffering
in the world.
Softcover 0-517-57635-X (1992)

LETTERS FROM A WILD STATE
Rediscovering Our True Relationship to Nature
by James G. Cowan

A luminous interpretation of Aboriginal spiritual
experience applied to the leading issue of our time:
the care of the earth.
Hardcover 0-517-58770-X (1992)